Lesekurs für Geisteswissenschaftler

Anhang Englisch

Reading Course for the Humanities
English Supplement

von

Marie-Luise Brandi und Barbara Momenteau

unter Mitwirkung der Verlagsredaktion

Klett Edition Deutsch

1.   Roots that are considered most productive*

Modern German vocabulary of Germanic and pre-Germanic origin seems to be entirely based, as is the case with Indo-European vocabulary in general, on monosyllabic roots consisting of two or three consonants. Given this limitation, the number of roots is relatively restricted so that most of the vocabulary must have been formed either by derivation (prefixes and suffixes) or composition. The Latin contribution (often via French), especially to scientific and literary vocabulary, is considerable. Greek has in principle only contributed to scientific vocabulary.

The most productive roots are enumerated here in the form of nouns (capital letter!), adjectives or adverbs, or of verb roots, with an indication of any vowel changes,
cf. 6: biegen – infinitive / – (biegt) 3rd pers. sg. present / bog – imperfect / gebogen – past participle,
   13: brechen – infinitive / bricht – 3rd pers. sg. present / brach – imperfect / gebrochen – past part.

1	acht	(to pay attention, be careful)
2	all	all/every
3	Arbeit	work, to work
4	bau	to build, cultivate
5	besser	better
6	bieg/-/o/o	to bend
7	biet/-/o/o	to offer
8	bild	to form
9	bind/-/a/u	to tie, bind
10	bitt/-/a/e	to ask, beg
(-	bleib	cf. leb 89)
11	blüh	to flourish
12	brauch	to use, need
13	brech/i/a/o	to break
14	breit	wide
15	brenn/-/a/a	to burn
16	bring/-/achte/acht	to bring
17	da	there
18	deck	to cover
19	denk/-/achte/acht	to think
	dank	
20	deut	to indicate, show
21	dien	to serve
22	Ding	thing
23	dreh	to turn
24	dring/-/a/u	to penetrate, press for
25	drück	to press
	druck	
26	dürf/a/u/u	to be allowed to
27	eigen	own
28	ein	one, a
29	Ende	end
30	ess/i/a/e	to eat

---

* according to Hanno Martin, linguist at the German Cultural Centre (Goethe-Institut), Munich

105	mög/a/ochte/ocht	to like, like to
106	Macht	power
	Mund	mouth
107	Mut	courage, spirits
108	na(c)h	after, near
109	Nacht	night
110	Name	name
111	nehm/imm/a/omm	to take
112	neu	new
113	(ge-)niess/–/o/o	to enjoy
	Genuß	enjoyment, pleasure
	nutz	to be of use, make use of
114	(ge-)nug	enough
115	offen	open
116	ordn	to (put in) order
117	pass	to pass, happen
118	(ge-)rade	straight, direct
119	rag	to rise, tower
	reg	to move
120	rat	to advise
121	Raum	space, room
122	Recht	right, law
	richt	to judge
123	Rede	speech
124	reich (1)	rich
125	reich (2)	to reach
126	reis	to travel
127	reiss/–/i/i	to pull, tear
128	riech/–/o/o	to smell
	rauch	to smoke
129	rinn/–/a/o	to run, flow
	renn/–/a/a	to run
130	rück (1)	to move (trans. and intrans.)
131	rück (2)	return, back
132	ruf/–/ie/u	to call, shout
133	Ruhe	quiet, calm
134	rühr	to stir, move
135	sag	to say
136	schaff/–/u/a	to create
137	schau	to look
138	(ge-)scheh/–/a/e	to happen, occur
	Geschichte	history, story
	schick	to send
139	scheid/–/ie/ie	to separate, divide
140	schein/–/ie/ie	to shine, seem
141	schieb/–/o/o	to push
	Schub	push
142	schiess/–/o/o	to shoot
	schütz	to protect
143	schlaf/ä/ie/a	to sleep
144	schlag/ä/u/a	to hit, strike, beat

145	schliess/–/o/o	to close, shut
	Schluß	end, conclusion
146	schneid/itt/itt	to cut
147	schreib/–/ie/ie	to write
148	schwer	heavy
149	seh/ie/a/	to see
	Sicht	sight, view
150	senk	to lower, sink
	sink/–/a/u	to sink (intrans.)
151	setz	to placc, sit, set
	sitz/–/aß/ess	to sit (intrans.)
152	soll	to be to (should)
	Schuld	debt, fault, guilt, obligation
153	spann	to stretch, tighten (trans.)
154	spiel	to play
155	sprech/i/a/o	to speak
	Spruch	saying, judgement
156	spreng	to blow up, break
	spring/–/a/u	to jump, leap
157	stech/i/a/o	to stick, pierce, sting
	steck	to put (in), stick
158	steh/–/and/and	to stand (intrans.)
	stell	to put, place, stand (trans.)
	Stadt	town
159	steig/–/ie/ie	to climb, go up
160	stimm	to tune
161	stoss/ö/ie/o	to push, knock
	Stoß	push, knock
162	streich/–/i/i	to stroke, spread
163	such	to search
164	Teil	part
165	trag/ä/u/a	to carry
166	treff/i/af/o	to hit, meet
167	treib/–/ie/ie	to drive, push
168	tret/itt/a/e	to step, tread
169	tun/–/tat/tan	to do
170	ü/ober	over, above, upper
171	unter	below, beneath, under
(–	verlier	cf. (ver-)lier 98)
172	wachs/ä/u/a	to grow
173	wäg	to weigh
	wieg/–/o/o	
	Gewicht	weight
174	wahr	true
175	wasch/ä/u/a	to wash
176	wechsel	to (ex)change
177	weich	soft
178	weit	wide, far
179	werb/i/a/o	to advertize, win
180	werf/i/a/o	to throw
	Wurf	throw

suffix	meaning	type of base-word	example
-tum	indicates a body of concepts a collective conduct gender: *neuter,* *except r Irrtum, r Reichtum*	nouns adjectives verbs	Christentum (Christianity) Eigentum (property) r Irrtum (error)
-ung	indicates an action in the sense of development towards a state; a phenomenon recalling its development gender: *feminine*	verbs	Unterscheidung (differentiation) Bewegung (movement)

2.2. Prefixes frequently used in the formation of nouns

prefix	meaning	type of base-word	example
Ge-	denotes 1. a collective sometimes with pejorative con- notations 2. the result of an action gender: *neuter, with a few exceptions,* *e.g. Gedanke*	nouns verbs	s Gebirge (mountains) s Gerede (gossip) s Gefüge (structure)
Miß-	(cf. prefixes used in the formation of verbs)		
Un-	expresses negation or turns the noun it is attached to into its opposite	nouns	e Unlust (displeasure)
Ur-	indicates authenticity or original character	nouns	e Ursache (cause)

2.3. Prefixes and suffixes frequently used in the formation of adjectives

prefixes	meaning	example
un-	expresses negation or turns the adjective it is attached to into its opposite	unmöglich (impossible)
ur-	intensifies the meaning, indicates authenticity or original character	uralt (very old)

12

suffixes	meaning	adjective root	example
-bar	expresses 1. that something is possible, can happen 2. that something or someone has a particular quality	verbs nouns	machbar (feasible) wunderbar (wonderful)
-haft	indicates a character, quality, aptitude	nouns adjectives verbs	beispielhaft (exemplary) krankhaft (sickly, pathological)
-ig	indicates a quality, state or similarity	nouns verbs adverbs	abhängig (dependent) heutig (today's)
-isch	indicates 1. origin 2. a quality (used for adjectives based on Greek or Latin roots) 3. something pejorative	nouns adjectives verbs	griechisch (Greek) kritisch (critical) logisch (logical) weibisch (effeminate)
-lich	indicates 1. particular qualities, an essential characteristic 2. that something is possible, can happen	nouns verbs adjectives	weiblich (feminine) verständlich (understandable)
-los	expresses deprivation, the absence of a quality (= "-less")	nouns	sinnlos (meaningless)
-sam	expresses through similarity 1. a quality 2. a tendency, a propensity	nouns verbs adjectives	langsam (slow) schweigsam (taciturn)

Indications of the comparative and superlative

(¨)er	indicates the comparative	ein älterer Text (an older text) älter sein als (to be older than)
(¨)st	indicates the superlative	der älteste Text (the oldest text) am ältesten sein (to be the oldest)

Note: There is frequently inflection in the comparative and superlative forms.

prefix	sep./insep.	meaning	example
um-	sep./insep	expresses a circular movement, a change of position of an object, a transformation	umgeben (to surround) um/stürzen (to overturn) um/gestalten (to alter)
ver-	insep.	expresses the intensification of an action, a transformation, sometimes to the extent that it denotes the opposite of the root word, i.e. has a negative meaning (root: nouns, adjectives and verbs)	versprechen (to promise) verbessern (to improve) verachten (to despise)
weiter-	sep.	expresses the continuation of an action	weiter/lesen (to read on)
wider-	sep./insep.	expresses hostility towards someone, and the reversal of a process wider = gegen = against	widersprechen (to contradict) widerlegen (to refute)
wieder-	sep./insep.	expresses repetition wieder = again	wiederholen (to repeat)
zer-	insep.	expresses dispersion, separation, destruction	zerstören (to destroy)
zu-	sep.	expresses 1. an act of closing 2. orientation, movement towards ... 3. an increase	zu/machen (to shut) zu/rufen (to shout sth to or at sb) zu/nehmen (to increase)
zurück	sep.	expresses return	zurück/kommen (to return)

3.   The verb

3.1.   General remarks on its form and function

The personal forms of the verb have more endings than they do in English. There are three which are particularly relevant for understanding texts in written German:

-t
-en
-e

There are, however, fewer tenses than there are in English. There is no verbal form that expresses the future. The principal tenses are:
1. The *present*, which covers the simple present and the present continuous in English and is also frequently used instead of the future.
2. The *imperfect*, which expresses something that belongs definitely to the past (though this may be a simple past or a past continuous in English).
3. The *perfect*, which expresses past events whose influence continues into the present.
   (N.B. The distinction between 2 and 3 is by no means so clearly made in German as it is in English.)
4. The *pluperfect*, which expresses something viewed in retrospect from a point in the past (the 'past in the past').

As in English, the formation of the imperfect (no. 2 in the above list) involves either the addition of a suffix, or a change in the vowel of the root, or (in a few cases) both. On this principle we distinguish between:
1. *'weak' verbs*, i.e. those which form the imperfect by the addition of a suffix, usually "-te".
2. *irregular verbs* which are divided into
   'strong' verbs, i.e. those which form the imperfect by changing the vowel of the root, and
   'mixed' verbs, i.e. those which change the vowel of the root and add a "-te" suffix.

The weak verbs have no vowel change:

infinitive	3rd sg. pres.	3rd sg. imperf.	past part.
machen	er macht	er machte	gemacht

The "-t-" between the root and the ending indicates the imperfect.

The strong verbs indicate the different tenses by means of a vowel change. There is no additional ending for the imperfect.

infinitive	3rd sg. pres.	3rd sg. imperf.	past part.
lesen	er liest	er las	gelesen

The mixed verbs have a vowel change but also take the endings of the weak verbs for the different tenses.

infinitive	3rd sg. pres.	3rd sg. imperf.	past part.
denken	er denkt	er dachte	gedacht

17

In German it is possible to express degrees of reality and indicate whether facts are real, hypothetical or unreal, or are facts to the truth of which the speaker is not committing himself. According to the speaker's interpretation of reality he will use:
- the indicative for *reality,*
- the imperfect subjunctive (Konjunktiv II) for *hypothesis* and *unreality,*
- the present subjunctive (Konjunktiv I) for *non-committal statements* (indirect speech).

The imperfect subjunctive corresponds in general to the use of the conditional in English. In the case of the irregular verbs it is often indicated by a vowel change:

> er kam – he came; er käme – he would come

The present subjunctive can also be used for final clauses:

> damit er verstehe – in order that he understand

or to express probability and possibility.

The present subjunctive of "sein" used with "auch" expresses concession:

> wie dem auch sei – be that as it may

There is no equivalent of its use for indirect speech in English. Since several of its forms are identical to the indicative, it is often the imperfect subjunctive that is found in indirect speech.

> Adorno sagt, daß die Menschen in der Gesellschaft isoliert seien (pres. subj.), weil sie keine Bindungen mehr hätten (imperf. subj.).
> Adorno says that people are isolated in society because they no longer have any ties.

As opposed to English, changing the introductory verb (sagt) into past tense (sagte) would have no effect on the subclauses of the above example.

To some extent, it is misleading that Konjunktiv I and II are usually referred to as present and imperfect subjunctive in English. These terms seem to imply that the subjunctive is connected to a tense rather than stressing that it is a mood.

3.2. Endings

ending	person	tense	type of verb	example
-T	3rd pers. sg. (2nd pers. pl.)*	present	all verbs except modal verbs and "wissen"	er machT er liesT
-EN	infinitive		all verbs	machEN, lesEN, wissEN
	1st pers. pl.	present/ imperfect	all verbs	wir schreibEN wir schriebEN
	3rd pers. pl.	present/ imperfect	all verbs	sie machEN sie machtEN

---

* Of minor importance for reading humanities texts.

ending	person	tense	type of verb	example
-E	1st pers. sg.	present	all verbs except modal verbs, "sein" and "wissen"	ich machE ich lesE
		imperfect	weak and mixed verbs	ich machtE ich dachtE, ich konntE
		present and perfect subjunctive	all verbs except the present sub-junctive of "sein"	ich machtE ich läsE ich wissE/ich wüßtE
	3rd pers. sg.	imperfect	weak and mixed verbs	er machtE er dachtE, er konntE
		present and imperfect subjunctive	all verbs except the present sub-junctive of "sein"	er machE, er machtE er lesE/er läsE er denkE/er dächtE er könnE/er könntE
-Ø	1st pers. sg.	present	modal verbs and "wissen"	ich kann- ich weiß-
	3rd pers. sg.	present	modal verbs and "wissen"	er kann- er weiß-
	1st pers. sg.	imperfect	strong verbs and "sein"	ich kam-, ich las- ich war-
	3rd pers. sg.	imperfect	strong verbs and "sein"	er kam-, er las- er war-
(-st	2nd pers. sg.)*			

3.3. The conjugation of the verbs "haben", "sein", "werden" and "wissen"

		haben	sein	werden	wissen
Present	ich	habe	bin	werde	weiß
	(du	hast	bist	wirst	weißt)
	er, sie, es	hat	ist	wird	weiß
	wir	haben	sind	werden	wissen
	(ihr	habt	seid	werdet	wißt)
	sie	haben	sind	werden	wissen
Imperfect	ich	hatte	war	wurde	wußte
	(du	hattest	wirst	wurdest	wußtest)
	er, sie, es	hatte	war	wurde	wußte
	wir	hatten	waren	wurden	wußten
	(ihr	hattet	wart	wurdet	wußtet)
	sie	hatten	waren	wurden	wußten
Past participle		gehabt	gewesen	geworden	gewußt

---

* Of minor importance for reading humanities texts.

3.4.   The past participle

The past participle indicates an acquired state, an action or a completed process.

How can a past participle be recognized?

The past participle is distinguished by the prefix "ge-" which precedes the verb root. In the weak and mixed verbs it ends with a "-t" and in the strong verbs with "-en" added to the verb root:

> ge ... t
> ge ... en

The prefix "ge-" may be placed in the middle of the past participle of a compound verb: where the verb has a separable prefix it comes between the prefix and the root of the verb.

infinitive		*past participle*
ausdrücken	(to express)	ausgedrückt
mitnehmen	(to take (with one))	mitgenommen

In the following cases "ge-" is omitted:

a) *compound verbs with an inseparable prefix,*

infinitive		*past participle*
erklären	(to explain)	erklärt
zerstören	(to destroy)	zerstört
verstehen	(to understand)	verstanden

b) *foreign verbs with an infinitive ending in "-ieren".*

infinitive		*past participle*
proklamieren	(to proclaim)	proklamiert
publizieren	(to publish)	publiziert

The use of the past participle

1. The past participle (uninflected) is used with the auxiliary "haben" or "sein" to form the perfect tense.
   In main clauses it goes to the end before the punctuation mark:

   > auxiliary .... past participle

   > 1910 hat Kandinsky sein erstes abstraktes Aquarell gemalt .
   > In 1910 Kandinsky painted his first abstract watercolour.
   >
   > 1914 ist Kandinsky nach Moskau zurückgegangen .
   > In 1914 Kandinsky returned to Moscow.

2. The past participle is used with the verb "werden" (indicating a process or development) to form the passive voice as opposed to the verb "sein" (indicating a state).

> Die Anwesenheit des Geistes in der Materie <u>wird geleugnet</u>.
> The presence of spirit in matter is denied.

3. Used <u>non-attributively it completes</u> the meaning of the verb <u>"sein"</u>. The attribute is uninflected.

> In der Materie ⊏ist⊐ der abstrakte Geist ⊏verborgen⊐.
> The abstract spirit is hidden in the matter.

4. The past participle can be used as an <u>adjective</u>.

   a) Used *attributively* it precedes the noun and agrees like an attributive adjective:

   > der <u>verborgene</u> Geist – the hidden spirit

   b) As a *substantival adjective* it is declined like an adjective:

   > das <u>Verborgene</u> – that which is hidden

   c) As an *adverb* it is uninflected:

   > Form und Inhalt sind nicht <u>getrennt</u> zu betrachten.
   > Form and content should not be considered separately.

5. Used in an <u>attributive participial phrase</u>, the past participle precedes the noun with which it agrees and is in turn preceded by any object or qualifying adjectives and adverbs it may have.

   > <u>Die</u> vom Künstler geprägten <u>Formen</u> sind zeitlich und relativ.
   >
   > <u>The forms</u> produced by the artist are temporal and relative.

6. Used as <u>a participial phrase following the noun to which it refers</u> the past participle follows the same regressive word order principle:

   > <u>Der Geist</u>, in der Materie verhüllt, spricht zur Seele des Menschen.
   >
   > <u>The spirit</u> hidden in matter speaks to man's soul.
   >
   > (This construction is a literary style.)

Points 4. to 6. also apply to the present participle.

<u>The present participle</u> can be recognized by the "-d" added to the infinitive:

> *infinitive*   *present participle*
> sprechen   (to speak)   sprechend (speaking)

Note: The present participle of the verb "sein" is only used as a noun: das "Seiende" (being). It is not used in attributive participial phrases.

3.5. List of frequent irregular verbs occurring particularly in the humanities

Infinitive	Imperfect	Perfect	English meaning
abhängen von	hing ... ab	hat abgehangen	to depend on
anfangen (fängt ... an)	fing ... an	hat angefangen	to start, begin
anwenden	wandte ... an	hat angewandt	to use, apply
bedenken	bedachte	hat bedacht	to think about, consider sth
befehlen (befiehlt)	befahl	hat befohlen	to order, command
beginnen	begann	hat begonnen	to start, begin, commence
begreifen	begriff	hat begriffen	to understand, grasp, comprehend
behalten (behält)	behielt	hat behalten	to keep, retain
beitragen (zu) (trägt bei)	trug ... bei	hat beigetragen	to contribute to
bekommen	bekam	hat bekommen	to get, receive, obtain
bergen (birgt)	barg	hat geborgen	to hold, hide, rescue
besitzen	besaß	hat besessen	to possess
bestehen (aus)	bestand	hat bestanden	to consist (of)
betreffen (betrifft)	betraf	hat betroffen	to concern, affect
beweisen	bewies	hat bewiesen	to prove, show
(sich) beziehen (auf)	bezog sich	hat sich bezogen	to refer to
bieten	bot	hat geboten	to offer
binden	band	hat gebunden	to tie, bind, unite
bitten	bat	hat gebeten	to ask, beg
bleiben	blieb	ist geblieben	to stay, remain
brechen (bricht)	brach	hat gebrochen	to break, overcome
brennen	brannte	hat gebrannt	to burn
bringen	brachte	hat gebracht	to bring, get, take
denken	dachte	hat gedacht	to think
dringen	drang	hat/ist gedrungen	to penetrate, press for
einwenden	wandte ... ein	hat eingewandt	to object to sth
empfangen (empfängt)	empfing	hat empfangen	to receive
empfehlen (empfiehlt)	empfahl	hat empfohlen	to recommend
empfinden	empfand	hat empfunden	to feel
enthalten (enthält)	enthielt	hat enthalten	to contain
entscheiden	entschied	hat entschieden	to decide
sich entschließen	entschloß	hat sich entschlossen	to decide, resolve, come to a decision
entsprechen (entspricht)	entsprach	hat entsprochen	to correspond (to)
entstehen	entstand	ist entstanden	to originate, emerge
erfahren (erfährt)	erfuhr	hat erfahren	to learn, experience
(sich) ergeben (ergibt)	ergab	hat ergeben	to result in, from
erkennen	erkannte	hat erkannt	to recognize, see, understand
erscheinen	erschien	ist erschienen	to appear, seem
erwägen	erwog	hat erwogen	to consider
erwerben (erwirbt)	erwarb	hat erworben	to acquire

22

Infinitive	Imperfect	Perfect	English meaning
fahren (fährt)	fuhr	ist gefahren	to go, drive, ride
fallen (fällt)	fiel	ist gefallen	to fall
fangen (fängt)	fing	hat gefangen	to catch
finden	fand	hat gefunden	to find
fließen	floß	ist geflossen	to flow
geben (gibt)	gab	hat gegeben	to give
gefallen (gefällt)	gefiel	hat gcfallen	to please
gehen	ging	ist gegangen	to go, walk
gelingen	gelang	ist gelungen	to succeed, be successful
gelten (gilt)	galt	hat gegolten	to be valid, count, be worth
genießen	genoß	hat genossen	to enjoy
geraten (gerät)	geriet	ist geraten	to get (into), fall into, come across, turn out
geschehen (geschieht)	geschah	ist geschehen	to happen, occur
gewinnen	gewann	hat gewonnen	to win, gain, obtain
greifen	griff	hat gegriffen	to seize, grasp
halten (hält)	hielt	hat gehalten	to hold, keep
hängen	hing	hat gehangen	to hang (intrans.)
heben	hob	hat gehoben	to lift, raise
heißen	hieß	hat geheißen	to call, name, be called, mean
helfen (hilft)	half	hat geholfen	to help
kennen	kannte	hat gekannt	to know
kommen	kam	ist gekommen	to come
laden (lädt)	lud	hat geladen	to load
lassen (läßt)	ließ	hat gelassen	to leave, let
laufen (läuft)	lief	ist gelaufen	to run, go
leiden	litt	hat gelitten	to suffer
lesen (liest)	las	hat gelesen	to read
liegen	lag	hat gelegen	to lie, be
meiden	mied	hat gemieden	to avoid
messen (mißt)	maß	hat gemessen	to measure
nachdenken	dachte ... nach	hat nachgedacht	to think about, reflect
nehmen (nimmt)	nahm	hat genommen	to take
nennen	nannte	hat genannt	to name, call
raten (rät)	riet	hat geraten	to advise, guess
reißen	riß	hat/ist gerissen	to tear, rip, pull
rufen	rief	hat gerufen	to call, shout
schaffen	schuf	hat geschaffen	to create
scheinen	schien	hat geschienen	to shine, seem, appear
schieben	schob	hat geschoben	to push, put (aside, off, into)
schlafen (schläft)	schlief	hat geschlafen	to sleep, be asleep
schlagen (schlägt)	schlug	hat geschlagen	to hit, beat, strike

Infinitive	Imperfect	Perfect	English meaning
schleichen	schlich	ist geschlichen	to sneak, steal, creep
schließen	schloß	hat geschlossen	to shut, close
schneiden	schnitt	hat geschnitten	to cut
schreiben	schrieb	hat geschrieben	to write
schreiten	schritt	ist geschritten	to stride, march on, walk
schweigen	schwieg	hat geschwiegen	to be silent
schwinden	schwand	ist geschwunden	to dwindle, fade
schwören	schwor	hat geschworen	to swear, take an oath
sehen (sieht)	sah	hat gesehen	to see
sein (ist)	war	ist gewesen	to be
senden	sandte	hat gesandt	to send
singen	sang	hat gesungen	to sing
sinken	sank	ist gesunken	to sink, decline
sitzen	saß	hat gesessen	to sit, be
sprechen (spricht)	sprach	hat gesprochen	to speak
springen	sprang	ist gesprungen	to jump, leap
stehen	stand	hat gestanden	to stand, be
steigen	stieg	ist gestiegen	to climb, go up
sterben (stirbt)	starb	ist gestorben	to die
stoßen (stößt)	stieß	hat/ist gestoßen	to push, knock
streichen	strich	hat gestrichen	to stroke, delete
streiten	stritt	hat gestritten	to argue, quarrel
tragen (trägt)	trug	hat getragen	to carry
treffen (trifft)	traf	hat getroffen	to hit, meet
treiben	trieb	hat getrieben	to drive, push, do
treten (tritt)	trat	hat getreten	to step, tread
trinken	trank	hat getrunken	to drink
tun	tat	hat getan	to do
übernehmen (übernimmt)	übernahm	hat übernommen	to take on, over
überwiegen	überwog	hat überwogen	to outweigh, predominate
verbergen (verbirgt)	verbarg	hat verborgen	to hide
verbieten	verbot	hat verboten	to forbid, ban, prohibit
vergessen (vergißt)	vergaß	hat vergessen	to forget, leave behind
vergleichen	verglich	hat verglichen	to compare
sich verhalten (verhält sich)	verhielt sich	hat sich verhalten	to behave
verlieren	verlor	hat verloren	to lose
verstehen	verstand	hat verstanden	to understand
vertreten (vertritt)	vertrat	hat vertreten	to replace, represent
verzeihen	verzieh	hat verziehen	to forgive, pardon
vorschlagen (schlägt vor)	schlug ... vor	hat vorgeschlagen	to suggest, propose
wachsen (wächst)	wuchs	ist gewachsen	to grow
weichen	wich	ist gewichen	to retreat, give way, move

Infinitive	Imperfect	Perfect	English meaning
weisen	wies	hat gewiesen	to show, point to
wenden	wandt	hat gewandt	to turn
werben (wirbt)	warb	hat geworben	to court
werfen (wirft)	warf	hat geworfen	to throw
wiegen	wog	hat gewogen	to weigh
winden	wand	hat gewunden	to wind, winch
ziehen	zog	hat gezogen	to pull, drag
zwingen	zwang	hat gezwungen	fo force

3.6. The modal verbs

Infin.	pres.	Imperf.	Perf.	meaning
dürfen	darf	durfte	hat gedurft	to be allowed to, may
können	kann	konnte	hat gekonnt	to be able to, know how to, be in a position to, can, may
mögen	mag	mochte	hat gemocht	denotes possibility or probability
(mögen as an autonomous verb				to like, like to
Note: vermögen + infinitive with "zu"				to be able to)
müssen	muß	mußte	hat gemußt	to have to, must: compulsion, necessity, inevitability
sollen	soll	sollte	hat gesollt	to be to, ought to, should
wollen	will	wollte	hat gewollt	to want, want to, wish to

"mögen", "können", "dürfen", "sollen", "müssen" are also used to express different degrees of probability:

das mag sein	that may be	eventuality
das kann so sein	that may be so	possibility
das dürfte wahr sein	that might be true	probability
das soll wahr sein	that is said to be true	probability according to rumour or report
das muß wahr sein	that must be true	almost a certainty

4.   Declensions

4.1.   General remarks

German has three genders, masculine, feminine and neuter, which are distinguished in the singular but have fallen together in the plural.

The declension of the noun has more or less disappeared, with the exception of nouns of Greek or Latin origin and the "-s" ending which indicates the genitive singular of masculine and neuter nouns.

> Die Aufgabe des Künstlers – the artist's task

The genitive "s" is also used with proper names.

> Kandinskys Malerei – Kandinsky's painting

The case of the noun is usually indicated by the article.

> Jede Form hat einen Inhalt – every form has content

When the article expresses the number, gender and case it is followed by the weak declension of the attributive adjective ("-e" / "-en").

> mit dem neuen Geist – with the new spirit

When there is no article in the noun phrase the attributive adjective takes the ending of the definite article to indicate number, gender and case.

> mit neuem Geist – with a new spirit

The adjective has no ending when it is used predicatively

> Inhalte sind absolut – contents are absolute

or as an adverb.

> Der Künstler ahmt die Natur frei nach – the artist freely imitates nature

4.2.   The definite article and the relative and demonstrative pronouns

	definite article	relative/demonstrative pronoun
deR	1. masc. nom. sg. 2. fem. dat. sg. 3. fem. gen. sg. 4. gen. pl.	1. masc. nom. sg. 2. fem. dat. sg. 3. fem. gen. sg. ---> deREN 4. gen. pl. ---> deREN
diE	1. fem. nom. sg. 2. fem. acc. sg. 3. nom. pl. 4. acc. pl.	1. fem. nom. sg. 2. fem. acc. sg. 3. nom. pl. 4. acc. pl.
daS	1. neut. nom. sg. 2. neut. acc. sg .	1. neut. nom. sg. 2. neut. acc. sg.
deN	1. masc. acc. sg. 2. dat. pl.	1. masc. acc. sg. 2. dat. pl. ---> deNEN
deM	1. masc. dat. sg. 2. neut. dat. sg.	1. masc. dat. sg. 2. neut. dat. sg.
deS	1. masc. gen. sg. 2. neut. gen. sg.	1. masc. gen. sg. ---> deSSEN 2. neut. gen. sg. ---> deSSEN

The following have the same declension as the definite article: the demonstrative pronouns "dieser", "jener", "solcher" and the interrogative and relative pronoun "welcher".

Declension of the definite article

Singular				Plural
	masc.	fem.	neut.	
nominative	der	die	das	die
accusative	den	die	das	die
dative	dem	der	dem	den
genitive	des	der	des	der

4.3. The indefinite article and the negative article "kein"

Indefinite article / negative article "kein"

(k)ein	1. masc. nom. sg. 2. neut. nom. sg. 3. neut. acc. sg.	

(k)einE	1. fem. nom. sg. 2. fem. acc. sg. 3. nom./acc. pl.	: keinE

(k)einEN	1. masc. acc. sg. 2. dat. pl.	: keinEN

(k)einEM	1. masc. dat. sg. 2. neut. dat. sg.	

(k)einER	1. masc. nom. sg. 2. fem. gen. sg. 3. fem. dat. sg. 4. gen. pl.	(when not accompanied by a noun: EinER muß es ja wissen! Someone must know it.) : keinER

(k)ein(E)S	1. neut. nom. sg. 2. neut. acc. sg. 3. masc. gen. sg. 4. neut. gen. sg.	(when not accompanied by a noun) (when not accompanied by a noun) : (k)einES : (k)einES

The indefinite article has no plural.
The following have the same declension as the negative article:

the possessive articles   mein (my)
[dein (your)]
sein (his, its)
ihr (her, its, their)
[unser (our)]
[euer (your)]

Declension of the indefinite and negative article

Singular				Plural
	masc.	fem.	neut.	
nominative	(k)ein	(k)eine	(k)ein	– / keine
accusative	(k)einen	(k)eine	(k)ein	– / keine
dative	(k)einem	(k)einer	(k)einem	– / keinen
genitive	(k)eines	(k)einer	(k)eines	– / keiner

4.4. The personal pronoun

ich	1st pers. nom. sg.	
mich	1st pers. acc. sg.	
mir	1st pers. dat. sg.	
du	2nd pers. nom. sg.	(forms rarely used in scientific texts)
dich	2nd pers. acc. sg.	
dir	2nd pers. dat. sg.	
er	3rd pers. masc. nom. sg.	
ihn	3rd pers. masc. acc. sg.	
ihm	1. 3rd pers. masc. dat. sg.	
	2. 3rd pers. neut. dat. sg.	
sie	1. 3rd pers. fem. nom. sg.	
	2. 3rd pers. fem. acc. sg.	
	3. 3rd pers. nom. pl.	> Sie: polite form of address
	4. 3rd pers. acc. pl.	
ihr	1. 3rd pers. fem. dat. sg.	
	2. 2nd pers. nom. pl.	
es	1. 3rd pers. neut. nom. sg.	
	2. 3rd pers. neut. acc. sg.	
wir	1st pers. nom. pl.	
uns	1. 1st pers. acc. pl.	
	2. 1st pers. dat. pl.	
euch	1. 2nd pers. acc. pl.	
	2. 2nd pers. dat. pl.	
ihnen	3rd pers. dat. pl.	– Ihnen: polite form

Note the similarity between the endings of the article and those of the personal pronoun in the third person:

Singular:				Plural
	masc.	fem.	neut.	
nominative	deR ein- eR	diE einE siE	daS ein- eS	diE — siE
accusative	deN eineN ihN	diE einE siE	daS ein- eS	
dative	deM eineM ihM	deR eineR ihR	deM eineM ihM	deN — ihneN

4.5. "es" and its function

The pronoun "es" has the following functions:

a) *personal pronoun*

> Das eindrucksvollste von allen Mitteln der Zerstörung ist das Feuer. Es ist weithin sichtbar.
> The most impressive of all the means of destruction is fire. It is visible from a long way off.

Note also: Die Pest hatte eine verheerende Wirkung. Sie tötete fast ein Drittel der Bevölkerung Mitteleuropas.
The pest had a devastating effect. It killed almost a third of the Central European population.

b) *demonstrative "es" used to refer back to a previous phrase or clause*

> Was mit einem in der Masse geschah ... war ebenso einschneidend wie rätselhaft. Es war ein Rätsel, das mich nicht mehr losließ.
> What happened to one in a crowd was as drastic as it was puzzling. It was a puzzle that I kept turning over in my mind.

c) *anticipatory "es"*

> Es war unmöglich, sich den Bildwerken in feindlicher Absicht zu nähern.
> ("es" announces or presents the infinitive phrase which follows)
> It was impossible to approach the statues with hostile intentions.

d) *"es" as the subject of impersonal phrases*

> Da es sich oft um Zerbrechliches handelt ...
> Since it is often a question of fragile things ...

e) *"es" as an introductory subject*

When for reasons of style another element cannot be placed at the beginning of a main or independent clause, "es" functions as an introductory subject.

> Es werden am liebsten Gegenstände zerstört.
> It is objects that people most like to destroy.

5.   Peculiarities of German orthography

Capital letters and punctuation marks are important aids to the understanding of a German text. All substantives – proper names and ordinary nouns – as well as adjectives, participles and infinitives used as nouns, begin with a capital letter.

Punctuation marks are used more or less in the same way as in English, with the exception of the comma. By contrast with English, the comma in German has a grammatical function: it is used to separate clauses. In addition, it separates the elements of an enumeration and divides off appositions.

Vowel modification ("Umlaut") can provide further clues to meaning:

    a   ---> ä
    o   ---> ö
    u   ---> ü
    au ---> äu

It is frequently used to change or specify the meaning of a word or root word:

a) *in the formation of plurals of nouns*

    Wort ---> Wörter

b) *in the formation of the comparative and superlative of adjectives*

    alt ---> älter ---> am ältesten

c) *where a word changes from one grammatical category to another*

    anders ---> ändern
    Macht ---> mächtig

d) *in the conjugation of irregular verbs*

    erfahren ---> er erfährt

   and in particular in the formation of the imperfect subjunctive

    wurde ---> würde
    war   ---> wäre.

6. The regressive structure of German

Contrary to English where sentences lead you from left to right from one piece of information to the next, the regressive structure of German forces you to read from right to left to obtain precise information. This regressive structure manifests itself at various levels:

– **The participial phrase**

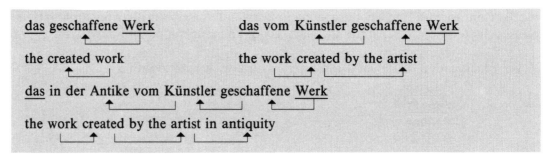

– **The verb phrase**

The verb phrase consists of the verb (which is rarely sufficient in itself)

Jede Form spricht.	Every form speaks.

and its complements which give meaning to the verb.

Der Geist spricht aus der Materie.	The spirit expresses itself in matter.

Der Geist ist verborgen.	The spirit is hidden.

The meaning of a verb may be completed by one or several complements, of which the most important comes last:

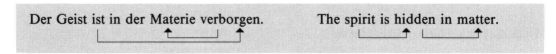

The following elements may be used to complete the meaning of the verb:

a) *an adverb or an attribute*

klar sprechen	to speak clearly

da sein	to be there

immer bestehen	to always exist

berühmt sein	to be famous

ein großer Künstler sein	to be a great artist

b) *a separable prefix*

<u>aus</u>drücken	to express

The verb phrase with a separable prefix usually has a second element completing the meaning of the verb which is hence the most important constituent of the verb phrase:

den <u>Geist</u> <u>aus</u>drücken	to express the spirit

c) *a noun*

die <u>Form</u> verkörpern	to embody the form
einer <u>Präzision</u> bedürfen	to be in need of precision
<u>Stellung</u> nehmen	to state one's position

d) *a prepositional phrase*

auf eine <u>Veränderung</u> <u>hin</u>weisen	to point out a change
<u>im 19. Jahrhundert</u> entstehen	to arise <u>in the 19th century</u>

e) *an infinitive with or without further complement*

<u>denken</u> können	to be able to think
<u>zu denken</u> vermögen	to be capable of thinking
die <u>Welt verändern</u> wollen	to want <u>to change the world</u>

Note: In the verb phrase with an infinitive the element which completes the meaning of the verb comes first before the infinitive, whereas English has the opposite word order.

– **The verb phrase in the clause**

By contrast with English, German separates the verb and the element which completes its meaning.

In a main or independent clause the conjugated verb is always in second place. The essential complement goes to the very end of the sentence. This construction forces you to read from right to left to obtain precise information (regressive structure!).

Kandinsky geht 1914 nach Moskau ¦ zurück.

Kandinsky <u>goes back to Moscow</u> in 1914.

In den meisten Fällen findet der Traum durch die Traumentstellung seine Aufklärung.

In most cases the dream <u>can be explained</u> by dream-distortion.

Note: The above examples are not rigidly binding. Other arrangements of the phrases are possible. For instance, the element which completes the meaning of the verb can be put at the end of a main clause for the purpose of emphasis (exbraciation – Ausklammerung) in the case of

a) *a prepositional phrase*

In den meisten Fällen ⌐findet⌐ der Traum ⌐seine Aufklärung⌐
durch die Traumentstellung.
In most cases <u>the dream is explained</u> by dream distortion.

b) *a dependent infinitive*

Er ⌐fängt⌐ ⌐an⌐ zu malen.   He begins to paint.

In the subordinate clause the conjugated verb comes last before the full stop or comma which marks the end of the clause. The verb phrase is thus brought together again at the end of the subordinate clause; if the verb has a separable prefix, this is joined to the verb again:

..., daß der Traum in den meisten Fällen durch die Traumentstellung
⌐seine Aufklärung⌐ ⌐findet⌐.
... that the dream <u>is</u> usually <u>explained</u> by dream-distortion.
..., als Kandinsky 1914 ⌐nach Moskau⌐ ⌐zurück geht⌐.
... when Kandinsky <u>goes back</u> to Moscow in 1914.

The infinitive phrase and the phrase introduced by "um" follow the same pattern:

Es ist schwer, auf diesem Gebiet zu ⌐neuen Erkenntnissen⌐ ⌐zu⌐ gelangen.
It is difficult to <u>make new discoveries</u> in this area.
Er schreibt, <u>um</u> die anderen ⌐von seinen Ansichten⌐ ⌐zu überzeugen⌐.
He writes <u>in order</u> to convince others <u>of his opinions</u>.

Note the importance of the comma in making a sentence easier to understand. It separates one clause from another:

Main clause, subordinate clause.
Subordinate clause, main clause.
Main clause part I, subordinate clause, main clause part II.
Subordinate clause, main clause part I, subordinate clause, main clause part II, subordinate clause.

A further characteristic of the word order

The conjugated verb comes first in three cases:

a) *in the case of a command*

<u>Erkennen</u> Sie dieses Prinzip!   Recognize this principle!

b) *in the case of a question*

<u>Erkennen</u> Sie dieses Prinzip?   Do you recognize this principle?

c) *in the case of a conditional clause where the conjunction "wenn" has been omitted for reasons of style*

> <u>Erkennen</u> Sie dieses Prinzip, <u>so</u>/<u>dann</u> verstehen Sie die ganze Theorie.
> If you recognize this principle you will understand the whole theory.

Note: A comparable construction is used in comparative clauses expressing unreality and introduced by "als ob"/"als wenn". "Ob" or "wenn" can be omitted and the conjugated verb then occupies the position of the conjunction:

> Es kam mir vor, <u>als</u> <u>ginge</u> es hier um etwas Wichtiges.
> Es kam mir vor, <u>als</u> <u>ob</u>/<u>als</u> <u>wenn</u> es hier um etwas Wichtiges <u>ginge</u>.
> It seemed to me that this was something important.

7.   Signal words

What we have termed "signal words" are words of different grammatical categories which are important and immediately obvious indications of the logical structure of a text, of the connection between phrases and of nuances of meaning.

7.1.   Signal words indicating the logical structure of a text

a) *the most frequent coordinating conjunctions (c.c.) and subordinating conjunctions (s.c.) and linking words with the same function*

Note: – The coordinating conjunctions (c.c.) do not affect the word order of the rest of the sentence.
  – After the subordinating conjunctions (s.c.) the conjugated form of the verb comes at the end of the subordinate clause.

They indicate

1. a link between two clauses of the same type	und (c.c.)	and
2. an alternative	oder (c.c.)	or
3. a correction or a contrast	aber (c.c.)	but
	(je)doch (c.c.)	yet, however
4. an explanation or a justification	weil (s.c.)	because
	da (s.c.)	as, since
	denn	for (because)
	nämlich	namely
	und zwar	and moreover, and what is more, and in fact, namely
5. a condition	wenn (s.c.)	if
	falls (s.c.)	if, in case
6. a consequence	so daß (s.c.)	so that
	deswegen deshalb	therefore, because of that, for that
	darum	that's why, because of that
	folglich	consequently, therefore
7. purpose	damit	in order that, so that
	um ... zu + infinitive	in order to
8. a question	ob (s.c.)	whether, if
9. a means	indem (c.s.)	by or through + gerund
	dadurch	thereby, because of this/that, through this/that

10. a contrast and a concession	obwohl (s.c.)	although (even) though
	obgleich (s.c.)	
	wenngleich (s.c.)	
	wenn ... auch	even though, even if
	trotzdem	nevertheless
11. a contrast	während (s.c.)	while, whereas
	anstatt ... zu + infin.	instead of
12. a restriction	soweit (s.c.)	as, as far as, in so far as
	insofern (s.c.)	inasmuch (as), in so far (as), if
13. a comparison denoting		
equality	wie	as, like
superiority	als	than
an unreal comparison	als ob (s.c.)	as if, as though
	als wenn (s.c.)	as if, as though
14. time	als (s.c.)	when (usually with the past tense)
	wenn (s.c.)	when (present and future)
	bevor (s.c.)	before
	nachdem (s.c.)	after
	während (s.c.)	while
	solange (s.c.)	as long as
	sobald (s.c.)	as soon as, (when) once
	seit (s.c.)	since
	seitdem (s.c.)	since
	bis (s.c.)	till, until; by the time
Indication of subordination without particular meaning		
	daß (c.s.)	that

Note: In addition to its three above functions as a signal word, "als" also means "as".

b) *demonstratives*

Most of these begin with "d". They take up a fact or a state already mentioned in the form of an antecedent or a clause or announce a state that will be defined more precisely in a complementary clause.

das	that
dieser, e, es	this, this one
jener, e, es	that, that one
so	thus, so
solcher, e, es	such
combinations of "da" + preposition:	
damit	with it, with that
dadurch	thereby, because of this/that, through this/that
darin	in that/it

dazu	to that/it
"dazu" followed by "daß" or "zu" + infinitive	to
darum	that's why, because of that
deshalb	therefore, because of that, for that
deswegen	therefore, because of that, for that

c) *certain interrogative pronouns*
   which raise fundamental questions in scientific texts:

was	what
wie	how
wozu	why
warum	why
weshalb	why
weswegen	why

d) *"pair elements"*, i.e. words which help to link two parts of a sentence together or promote rhetorical balance.
   They include correlatives in the proper sense of the term and other word combinations of a correlative nature.

They indicate:
coordination

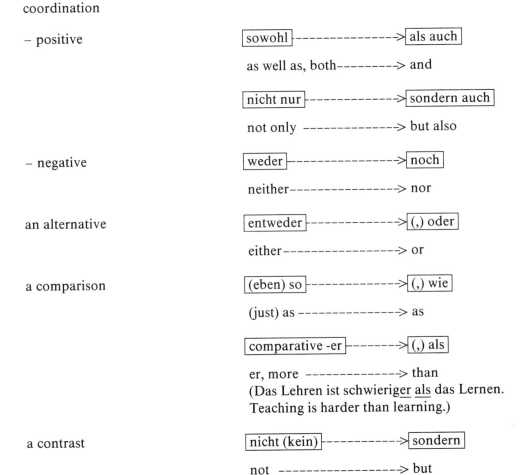

– positive

sowohl -----------------> als auch

as well as, both---------> and

nicht nur ------------->sondern auch

not only -------------> but also

– negative

weder ----------------->noch

neither---------------> nor

an alternative

entweder ------------->(,) oder

either----------------> or

a comparison

(eben) so ------------->(,) wie

(just) as -------------> as

comparative -er------->(,) als

er, more -------------> than
(Das Lehren ist schwieriger <u>als</u> das Lernen.
Teaching is harder than learning.)

a contrast

nicht (kein) ---------->sondern

not ----------------> but

a contrast, a concession

einerseits ------------> (,) andererseits

on the one hand ------> on the other hand

zwar ----------------> aber/doch

certainly -------------> but

wenn ... auch ---------> so ... doch

even though ----------> still

(Wenn er auch viel weiß, so weiß er doch nicht alles.
Even though he knows a lot, he still does not
know everything.)

mögen + auch --------> (so) ... doch

however, (whatever)
no matter ------------> still

(Mag er auch viel wissen, er weiß doch nicht alles.
No matter what he knows he still does not know
everything.)

mögen + noch so ------> , (doch)

(n)ever so, however,
no matter -------------> still, but

(Er mag noch so viel wissen, er weiß doch nicht alles.
However much he knows, he still does not know everything.)

a consequence

so + adjective --------> , daß

so + adjective ---------> that

(Das ist so kompliziert, daß man es nicht verstehen
kann.
That is so complicated that it cannot be understood.)

je + comparative ------> um so/desto + comparative

the more/the less ------> the more/the less

(Je mehr man sich umsieht, um so/desto besser versteht
man die Menschen.
The more one looks round, the better one understands
people.)

wenn ----------------> so/dann

if --------------------> (then)

a restriction

insofern ------------> als

inasmuch ------------> as
in so far -------------> as

the announcement
– of a fact

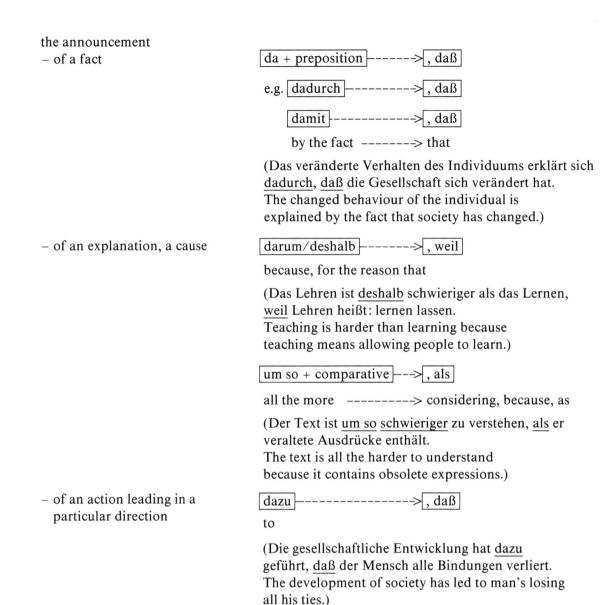

| da + preposition | ------> | , daß |

e.g. | dadurch | ---------> | , daß |

| damit | ----------> | , daß |

by the fact -------> that

(Das veränderte Verhalten des Individuums erklärt sich dadurch, daß die Gesellschaft sich verändert hat.
The changed behaviour of the individual is explained by the fact that society has changed.)

– of an explanation, a cause

| darum/deshalb | -------> | , weil |

because, for the reason that

(Das Lehren ist deshalb schwieriger als das Lernen, weil Lehren heißt: lernen lassen.
Teaching is harder than learning because teaching means allowing people to learn.)

| um so + comparative | ---> | , als |

all the more ---------> considering, because, as

(Der Text ist um so schwieriger zu verstehen, als er veraltete Ausdrücke enthält.
The text is all the harder to understand because it contains obsolete expressions.)

– of an action leading in a
  particular direction

| dazu | ----------------> | , daß |

to

(Die gesellschaftliche Entwicklung hat dazu geführt, daß der Mensch alle Bindungen verliert.
The development of society has led to man's losing all his ties.)

7.2. Signal words modifying the statement of a sentence (i.e. adverbs)

They are placed
– before the element that completes the meaning of the verb, thus changing the statement of the whole sentence,
– before the element of the clause that is exclusively affected by the modification.
These adverbs, placed before the element which determines the meaning of the verb, invalidate or confirm the statement of the clause and range from complete negation to confirmation.

a) *negation*

nicht	not
überhaupt nicht/gar nicht	not at all
noch nicht	not yet
nicht mehr	no more
nie/niemals	never

40

nirgends/nirgendwo	nowhere
niemand/keiner (pronoun)	no-one, nobody
kein (negative article)	no
kein ... mehr	no more
ohne (preposition)	without

b) *restriction*

nur/bloß/allein	only, alone
kaum	scarcely, hardly, barely
selten	rarely, seldom
wenig	little
immerhin	all the same, anyhow, at any rate

c) *coordination*

auch	also, too
ebenfalls/gleichfalls	as well, likewise, also
zugleich	at the same time

d) *probability to certainty*

vielleicht	perhaps
wohl	probably, no doubt, perhaps, possibly
wahrscheinlich	probably
anscheinend	apparently
offenbar	obviously, apparently, evidently
oft/häufig	often, frequently
sicher	of course, surely, certainly
gewiß	certainly, surely
bestimmt	definitely, certainly
zweifellos	undoubtedly
immer	always

More subjective adverbs expressing probability/certainty:

möglicherweise	possibly
eher	rather, sooner, more likely
vermutlich	presumably, probably
jedenfalls	anyhow, in any case, at least, at any rate
eigentlich	actually, really, anyway
wirklich	really

Note: For the sake of clarity in this reading method we have regrouped the signal words and not always kept to traditional grammatical categories. They have in addition been selected on the basis of frequency in humanities texts.

7.3.   Signal words in alphabetical order

		page
aber	but	36
allein	only, alone	41
als	than	37
als	when	37
als ob	as if, as though	37

8. Development and state in German

In German importance is attached to the expression of development on the one hand and state on the other at various grammatical levels and to a description of the transition between the two.

8.1. From "werden" to "sein"

In this context, the verb "werden" plays an important part. By comparison with "sein", which expresses a state, "werden" describes <u>development, a process</u>, the result of which is indicated by its complement.

a) *"werden" + attribute = development towards a state ("to become")*

> Die geistigen Erzeugnisse der einzelnen Nationen <u>werden</u> <u>Gemeingut</u>.
> The intellectual products of the individual nations become common property.
>
> Die bürgerlichen Verhältnisse <u>sind</u> <u>zu eng geworden</u>.
> Bourgeois conditions have become too restricted.

"werden" + zu + attribute = development leading to a transformation, sometimes associated with a negative outcome

> Philosophie heißt: auf dem Wege sein. Ihre Fragen sind wesentlicher als ihre Antworten, und jede Antwort <u>wird</u> <u>zur</u> <u>neuen Frage</u>.
> Philosophy always leads onwards. Its questions are more important than its answers and every answer becomes a new question.
>
> Die Behauptung des Individuums in der Gesellschaft <u>ist</u> <u>zu</u> <u>einem fast unlösbaren Problem</u> <u>geworden</u>.
> Man's assertion of himself as an individual in society has become an almost insoluble problem.

b) *"werden" + infinitive = the probability of an action or a a state of fact / intention of carrying out an action ("future")*

> Mit ihren schwieligen Händen <u>werden</u> sie (die Kommunisten) erbarmungslos alle Marmorstatuen der Schönheit <u>zerbrechen</u>, die meinem Herzen so teuer sind.
> With their callused hands they (the communists) will mercilessly smash all the marble statues of beauty that are so dear to my heart. (Heine)

c) *"werden" + past participle = a process that is taking place / development towards a state or an accomplished fact (passive voice)*

> Das, was früher der Geist war, <u>wird</u> heute mit dem Intellekt <u>identifiziert</u>. (present)
> What was formerly spirit is today identified with the intellect.
>
> Früher <u>wurden</u> diese Prinzipien (Vater=Geist, Mutter=Materie) in vielfältiger Weise rituell <u>verehrt</u>. (imperfect)
> Formerly these principles (father=spirit, mother=matter) were ritually venerated in a number of different ways.

> In dem Maß, wie unser wissenschaftliches Verständnis zugenommen hat, ist unsere Welt <u>entmenschlicht</u> <u>worden</u>. (perfect)
> As our scientific understanding has increased, our world has been correspondingly dehumanized.

The verb "sein" expresses <u>a state</u>. Used with a past participle as a complement it expresses an acquired state.

> In der Materie <u>ist</u> der abstrakte, schaffende Geist <u>verborgen</u>.
> The abstract, creative spirit is hidden in matter.
>
> Die Zeit <u>ist</u> weitgehend von materialistischer Weltanschauung <u>beherrscht</u>.
> The age is largely dominated by a materialistic world view.

Note the differences!

development/process	*state/acquired state*
Er <u>wird</u> alt. He is growing old.	Er <u>ist</u> alt. He is old.
Er <u>wird</u> Professor. He is going to be a professor.	Er <u>ist</u> Professor. He is a professor.
Die Zeit <u>wird</u> vom Materialismus <u>beherrscht</u>. The age is becoming marked by materialism.	Die Zeit <u>ist</u> vom Materialismus <u>beherrscht</u>. The age is marked by materialism.
Die Zeit <u>wurde</u> vom Kolonialsmus <u>geprägt</u>. The age became dominated by colonialism.	Die Zeit <u>war</u> vom Kolonialismus <u>geprägt</u>. The age was dominated by colonialism.

8.2.   From process to result in the formation of nouns derived from verbs

The same need to distinguish the stages between the process itself and the acquired state can be seen in the formation of nouns.

a) The process in itself, presented as a phenomenon, is expressed by the *infinitive used as a noun*. These nouns are particularly to be found in philosophy where concepts must be differentiated more precisely. However, they are equally part of everyday language.

das Leben	life
das Schweigen	silence
das Wissen	knowledge
das Denken	thinking, thought
das Nachdenken	thought, reflection
das Wesen	nature, essence, being
das Sein	being, essence, existence, life
das Dasein	existence, life, presence
das Geschehen	happenings, events
das Wollen	volition

das Lernen	learning
das Suchen	search
das Philosophieren	philosophizing
das Lesen	reading

b) Action in the sense of development towards a state is expressed by *the suffix "-ung"*. These nouns represent a phenomenon recalling its development and are therefore particularly to be found in psychology. However, their current use in everyday language seems to prove the need to express the inherent developmental character of the phenomenon named.

die Bedeutung	meaning, importance, significance
die Beschäftigung	activity, occupation
die Behandlung	treatment
die Bedingung	condition, requirement
die Erinnerung	memory
die Übertragung	transference
die Verdrängung	repression
die Anpassung	adaptation, adjustment
die Selbstbehauptung	self-assertion, self-assertiveness
die Enstehung	emergence, origination, genesis, formation
die Entwicklung	development, evolution
die Unterdrückung	suppression
die Bewußtwerdung	dawning of consciousness
die Vorstellung	idea, concept, notion, imagination

c) The result of a process that has in some way become institutionalized is expressed by
   - *derivatives of verb-stems without the addition of a suffix*
   - *nouns derived from verbs with the suffix "-nis"*
   The language of philosophy and sociology utilizes these nouns as opposed to those which express a process in themselves ("-en") and those which designate the transition between process and acquired state ("-ung").

der Begriff	concept, term
der Ursprung	origin
der Anspruch	claim, right, demand, pretension
der Einfluß	influence
der Vorzug	advantage, merit
der Fortschritt	progress, advance
der Gedanke*	thought, idea, concept
der Inhalt	content(s)
der Vorgang	proceedings, event, process
der Zustand	state, condition
der Druck	pressure
der Zwang	compulsion, obligation
das Maß	measure, measurement
das Verbot	ban, prohibition

Note: Because of the many nouns that are formed from irregular verbs it is useful to know the vowel changes of the various tenses.

---

* the "-e" in "Gedanke" is not a suffix

Derivatives of verb roots with the suffix "-nis":

das Ergebnis	result, outcome
das Geschehnis	event, incident
das Verständnis	understanding, comprehension
das Hindernis	obstacle, hindrance
das Wagnis	risk
das Bündnis	alliance, league
die Erlaubnis	permission
die Kenntnis	knowledge

Note the difference:

verb in the infinitive	the process as a phenomenon (infinitive used as a noun)	phenomenon recalling its development (verb-stem + "-ung")	result/institution (derived from the verb-stem without suffix or with "-nis")
erkennen (to recognize)	das Erkennen (recognition, identification, perception)	/	die Erkenntnis (realization, knowledge, cognition, perception)
unterscheiden (to differentiate)	das Unterscheiden (distinction, differentiation)	die Unterscheidung (distinction, differentiation)	der Unterschied (difference)
erscheinen (to appear, seem)	das Erscheinen (appearance)	die Erscheinung (appearance, apparition, phenomenon)	/
binden (to bind)	(rare)	die Bindung (tie, link, bond)	das Band (tie, bond, link) der Bund (federation) das Bündnis (alliance, league)
sich verhalten (to behave)	das Verhalten (behaviour)	/	das Verhältnis (relation)
sich beziehen auf (to refer to, relate to)	(rare)	die Beziehung (relation)	der Bezug (reference)

The use of the *present participle* and the *past participle used as a noun* is a phenomenon parallel to that described above: the present participle expresses movement, something that is happening, while the past participle indicates the result of an action, something that has been acquired.

Present participles used as nouns are found in philosophy, past participles in philosophy and in literature.

48

das Seiende	being
das Werdende	that which is developing, nascent
das Kommende	that which is coming
das Bestehende	that which exists
das Bleibende	that which remains
das Entscheidende	that which is decisive, crucial
das Schwerwiegende	that which is serious
das Folgende	that which follows
das Gewesene	the past, what was before
das Gewordene	that which has developed
das Gebliebene	that which has remained
das Entschiedene	that which has been decided
das Erlebte	actual experience
das Unbewußte	the unconscious
das Verborgene	the hidden
das Erkannte	that which has been recognized, known
etwas Verschiedenes	something different
etwas Vorgegebenes	something given

8.3.   "zu" as the indicator of movement in a particular direction

"zu" expresses a direction, a tendency towards, even an intention (with the exception of "zu" + adjective or adverb = "too much"...).

a) *the preposition "zu" = to, towards can also express purpose*

Durch den Widerstand lenkt das Es des Kranken die Behandlung des Artzes <u>zum</u> Guten oder <u>zum</u> Bösen.
By resistance, the Id of the patient gives the treatment of the doctor a favourable or an unfavourable turn.

Der Wille <u>zur</u> Macht
The will for power = aiming at power

Doch was bringst du uns <u>zum</u> Geschenke?
But what present are you bringing us? = what are you bringing in order to offer it to us as a present?

b) *"zu" in an infinitive phrase = a tendency, an activity that is being aimed at*

Das Es ... sucht, sobald als möglich, zu seinen gewohnten Ausdrucksformen des gesunden Lebens zurück<u>zu</u>kehren.
The Id tries to return as soon as possible to its normal forms of expression with the body in a state of health.

Das Es hat Gewohnheiten, in denen es <u>zu</u> leben und <u>zu</u> handeln liebt.
The Id has ways in which it prefers to live and act.

c) *"zu" preceded by "um" = expression of purpose in an infinitive phrase*

> Das Es greift in die Außenwelt hinein, <u>um</u> krank <u>zu</u> werden.
> The Id has recourse to the external world, in order to become ill.

d) *"zu" as a separable verbal prefix = motion towards*

> Der Kranke <u>geht</u> nur ungern auf den Arzt <u>zu</u>.
> The patient only approaches the doctor with reluctance.
>
> Er geht häufig nur zu ihm, weil irgendwelche Leute ihm ... <u>zureden</u>.
> He frequently only goes to him because he is persuaded to by other people.

e) *"zu" as a preposition belonging to certain verbs = motion towards / intention (up to the point of actual transformation)*

> Der Patient möchte den Arzt <u>dazu</u> <u>bringen</u> zu urteilen und zu verurteilen.
> The patient would like to bring the doctor to the point of judging and condemning.
>
> In der Philosophie wird jede Antwort <u>zur</u> neuen Frage.
> In philosophy every answer becomes a new question.

Note: As interrogative and demonstrative pronouns the signal words "wozu" and "dazu" express intention or purpose.

8.4. The different aspects of development expressed by verb prefixes

The considerable number of verb prefixes in German would seem to accord with the need to differentiate between the various nuances of development and accomplishment of an action.

a) The *beginning* of an action can be indicated by:

> "an-" : anfangen (to begin)
> "ent-" : entstehen (to originate, arise, emerge)
> "er-" : erblühen (to blossom)

b) The *duration and intensification* of an action which can lead to a *transformation* can be indicated by:

> *duration, intensification:*
> "weiter-" : weiterlesen (to read on)
> "an-"   : andauern (to continue, last)
>   anhalten (to last)
> "be-"   : behalten (to keep)
> "ver-"   : verurteilen (to condemn)
> "zu-"   : zunehmen (to increase)
> "über-"   : übertreiben (to exaggerate, go too far)

for change:

"um-"   :   umgestalten (to alter, reorganize)
"ver-"   :   vergöttern (deify, idolize)
              verachten (despise, scorn)

c) The *result* of an action or the *finality* of it can be indicated by:

"durch-" :   durchführen (to carry out)
"auf-"   :   auflösen (to dissolve)
"aus-"   :   ausführen (to carry out, execute)
"er-"   :   erreichen (to reach, attain)
"zer-"   :   zerbrechen (to break, smash)

d) *Certain prefixes cover several aspects of the process of the action. The most representative are "er-" and "ver-".*

"er-"   indicates embarking on an action or entering a state which can lead to an intensification brought about by this process and extend to the accomplishment of the action, in other words indicate the result obtained:

erblühen (to blossom)	erleichtern (to make easier)
ersuchen (to request)	erkennen (to recognize, identify)
erreichen (to reach, obtain)	

"ver-"   expresses an intensification of the action, a transformation sometimes leading to the opposite sense of the word without the prefix, i.e. a negative sense:

vergehen (pass = time which passes)	verkörpern (to embody)
verbessern (to improve)	verbrennen (to burn)
verkennen (to misjudge, underestimate)	

9.   Common abbreviations

a.a.O.	am angegebenen Ort	loc. cit.
Abb.	Abbildung	illustration, diagram
Abt.	Abteilung	dept.
Anm.	Anmerkung	note
Aufl.	Auflage	edition, circulation
Bd./Bde	Band/Bände	vol(s).
Begr.	Begriff	concept, term, idea
bes.	besonders	in particular
Best.-Nr.	Bestellnummer	order number or code
betr.	betreffend, betreffend	concerning, re.
Bez.	Bezeichnung	designation, term
bzw.	beziehungsweise	or, respectively or that is to say
ca.	circa	approx.
dass.	dasselbe	the same, idid
ders.	derselbe	the same, ibid
d.h.	das heißt	i.e.
d.i.	das ist	i.e.
ebd.	ebenda	ibid., ibidem
entspr.	entsprechend	corresponding, correspondingly, corresponding to
ev./evtl.	eventuell	possibly
f./ff.	und die folgende(n) Seite(n)	f./ff.
Ggs.	Gegensatz	(by) contrast
Hg./Hrsg.	Herausgeber	ed. (editor)
hg./hgg./hrsg. von	herausgegeben von	ed. (edited by)
i.a.	im allgemeinen	in general
i.J.	im Jahre	in the year, p.a. (per annum)
Jahrg./Jg.	Jahrgang	year
Jh.	Jahrhundert	century
Kap.	Kapitel	chapter
lat.	lateinisch	Latin
m.E.	meines Erachtens	in my opinion
n.Chr.	nach Christus	A D
Nr.	Nummer	No., no. (number)
o.	oben/oder	above/or
od.	oder	or
o.e.	oben erwähnt	above-mentioned
o.g.	oben genannt	above-mentioned
o.J.	ohne Jahr	without /no publication year
S.	Seite(n)	p., pp.
s.	siehe	see
s.a.	siehe auch	see also
s.o.	siehe oben	see above
s.u.	siehe unten	see below
sog./sogen.	sogenannt	as it is called, so-called
Tab.	Tabelle	tab.
Taf.	Tafel	table

u.	und/unten	and/below
u.a.	und andere	and others
	unter anderem/n	among other things
u.ä.	und ähnliche(s)	and the like
u.a.m.	und anderes mehr	and more besides
usw.	und so weiter	etc., and so on
u.Z.	unserer Zeitrechnung	A D
v.	von	by
v. Chr.	vor Christus	B C
v.u.Z.	vor unserer Zeitrechnung	B C
Verf.	Verfasser	author
vgl./vergl.	vergleiche	cf. (confer, compare)
Vlg./Verl.	Verlag	publishing house
Wörterb.	Wörterbuch	dictionary
z.B.	zum Beispiel	e.g. (for example)
z.T.	zum Teil	in part
Zschr./Zts./Ztsch.	Zeitschrift	periodical, magazine, journal, bulletin

10.   Frequent words

10.1.   Words occurring frequently in philosophical texts

e	Abfolge	succession, sequence
e	Abgrenzung	delimitation, definition
e	Abhängigkeit	dependence, dependency
e	Absicht	intention, purpose
e	Allgemeingültigkeit	universal or general validity
		universality, generality
e	Anerkennung	recognition, acceptance
e	Annahme	assumption, acceptance
e	Anschauung	view, opinion, idea, intuition
	e Anschauungsweise	approach, point of view, viewpoint
r	Anspruch	claim, right, demand, pretension
e	Auffassung	comprehension, conception, view
e	Aufklärung	enlightenment, Enlightenment, elucidation
	aufgeklärt	enlightened, well-informed
r	Ausdruck	expression
e	Auseinandersetzung	explanation, exposition
		argument, conflict
r	Ausgang	exit, point of departure, outcome
e	Bedeutung	meaning, importance, significance
e	Bedingung	condition, requirement
s	Begreifen (begreifen)	comprehension, apprehension, conception (to understand, to comprehend)
r	Begriff	concept term, idea
e	Begründung	foundation, reasons, justification
e	Behauptung	assertion, statement
e	Beherrschung	domination, control
e	Bemühung um	effort, endeavour (to, towards)
e	Beschaffenheit	constitution, quality
e	Besinnung	contemplation, reflection
s	Bestehende (bestehen)	that which exists (to exist)
e	Bestimmung	destination, determination, (description in philos. but rare)
e	Betrachtung	contemplation, consideration
e	Beurteilung	judgement, opinion, assessment
r	Beweis	proof, argument, demonstration
e	Bewußtmachung	process of making something conscious (to someone)
	(bewußt machen)	(to make something conscious)
s	Bewußtsein	consciousness, awareness
	(sich einer Sache bewußt sein)	(to be conscious, aware of something)
s	Bewußtwerden	awareness
	(sich einer Sache bewußt werden)	(to become conscious, aware of something)
e	Bewußtwerdung	dawning of consciousness
e	Bezeichnung	designation, appellation
e	Bildung	formation, education

e	Darstellung	representation
s	Dasein	existence, presence
s	Denken	thinking, thought
e	Deutung	interpretation
s	Ding	thing, substance, entity
	s Dinghafte	that which is real, objective, tangible
	s Dinghaftmachung	reification; the process of making something real, objective
	s Dingliche	that which is real
s	Eigentliche	that which is actual, real, proper essential
e	Eigentlichkeit	authentic being, essentiality
e	Eigenschaft	quality, property, characteristic
e	Einbildung	imagination, illusion
r	Eindruck	impression
e	Einheit	unity
e	Einrichtung	institution, establishment
e	Einschränkung	limitation
e	Einsicht	insight, understanding, discernment
e	Einwand	objection
e	Entstehung	emergence, origination, genesis, formation
e	Entwicklung	development, evolution
e	Erfahrung	experience, empiricism
s	Erfassen (erfassen)	grasp, understanding, comprehension (to grasp, understand, comprehend)
s	Ergebnis (sich ergeben)	result, consequence (to result, arise from)
s	Erkennen (erkennen)	cognition, process of identification (to know, (re)cognize, perceive)
	e Erkenntnis	knowledge, cognition, perception, intuition
e	Erklärung	explanation
s	Erleben (erleben)	the process of experiencing, living through sth (to experience)
	s Erlebnis	experience, event, adventure
	s Erlebte	actual experience
e	Erscheinung	appearance, phenomenon
e	Erwägung	consideration
e	Erzeugung	production
r	Fortschritt (fortschreiten)	progress (to progress)
r	Gedanke	thought, idea, concept
	r Gedankengang	train of thought, sequence of ideas
s	Gefüge	structure, framework, system
r	Gegensatz	antithesis, contrast, opposite
r	Gegenstand	object
s	Gegenteil	contrary
e	Gegenüberstellung	opposition, comparison
e	Gegenwart	present
r	Geist (geistig)	spirit, mind (spiritual)
	gelten	to be valid
s	Gemüt (cf. Mut)	disposition, mind
s	Geschehen	happenings, events

e	Geschichte	history
e	Gesetzmäßigkeit	regularity, legitimacy
r	Gesichtspunkt	point of view
e	Gesinnung	sentiments, convictions
s	Gewissen	conscience
e	Größe	size, quantity, significance
r	Grund	bottom, base, reason
	e Grundlage	basis, foundation, fundamentals
	r Grundsatz	principle, axiom, postulate, rule
e	Gültigkeit	validity
r	Inhalt	content(s)
e	Kenntnis	knowledge
e	Kunst	art
	(künstlerisch, künstlich)	(artistic, artificial)
e	Meinung	opinion
r	Mut (cf. Gemüt)	spirits, mood
s	Nichts	nothingness, negation of being, nonentity
e	Ordnung	order, system
s	Recht	right
	e Rechtfertigung	justification
e	Richtung	direction, trend
e	Sache	thing, object, matter
	e Sachlichkeit	objectivity
	r Sachverhalt	circumstances, facts
s	Schicksal	fate, destiny
e	Seele	soul, psyche, mind
s	Seiende	being
s	Sein	being, essence, existence, life
	e Seinsweise	way of being
r	Sinn	sense, meaning
	e Sinnesart	way of thinking
e	Sitte(n)	customs, mores, morals
	sittlich	moral, ethic(al)
	e Sittlichkeit	morality, morals
	e Sittenlehre	ethics, moral philosophy
r	Standpunkt	point of view, position
e	Stimmung	mood, humour, state of mind
r	Streit	controversy
	s Streitgespräch	debate, disputation
e	Tatsache	fact
	e Tatsächlichkeit	actuality, fact
e	Übereinstimmung	correspondence, congruence, indicalness, identicality

e	Überlegung	consideration, deliberation, reflection
e	Überzeugung	conviction(s)
e	Unterscheidung	differentiation, distinction
r	Unterschied	difference, distinction
e	Untersuchung	investigation, examination
e	Ursache	cause, reason
r	Ursprung	origin, source
s	Urteil	judgement, proposition
e	Verallgemeinerung	generalization
s	Verfahren	process, procedure
e	Vergangenheit	past
r	Verlauf	course, development
e	Vermutung	supposition, assumption, hypothesis
e	Vernunft	reason, intellect
e	Verschiedenheit	difference, different nature
r	Verstand (verstehen)	mind, intellect
		understanding, reason (to understand)
s	Verständnis	understanding
e	Voraussetzung	premise, condition, assumption, presupposition
r	Vorgang	proceedings, event, process
r	Vorgehen (vorgehen)	procedure, proceeding (to proceed)
e	Vorstellung	idea, concept, notion
r	Wahnsinn	madness, insanity
e	Wahrheit	truth
e	Welt	world
	weltlich	worldly, mundane, secular
e	Weltanschauung	world view
s	Werden	becoming
r	Wert	value, importance
e	Wertung	evaluation, assessment
e	Wertgröße	order of value
s	Wesen (wesentlich)	nature, essence, being (essential)
e	Wesenheit	being, entity
r	Widerspruch	contradiction, inconsistency
r	Wille	will, volition
e	Willkür (willkürlich)	arbitrariness (arbitrary)
e	Wirklichkeit	reality
s	Wissen	knowledge
e	Wissenschaft	science
s	Zeichen	sign
e	Bezeichnung (bezeichnen)	designation (to designate)
r	Zusammenhang	connection, context, coherence
r	Zustand	state, condition

10.2. Words occurring frequently in psychology texts

r	Ablauf	course, development
e	Abhängigkeit	dependency
e	Ableitung (ableiten)	derivation, deduction (to infer, derive, deduce)
s	Abreagieren (sich abreagieren)	catharsis, abreaction, acting out (to abreact, act out)
e	Absicht	intention, purpose
e	Abwehr	defence
	Abwehrmechanismen (pl.)	defence or escape mechanisms, defence activity
r	Affekt	affect, emotion
r	Anfall	attack, fit, seizure
e	Angst	anxiety, fear, phobia
	r Angstzustand	state of anxiety
e	Anpassung	adaptation, adjustment, accommodation
r	Anspruch	aspiration, claim, pretence
r	Antrieb	drive, impulse
r	Archetyp(us)	archetype
s	Band	tie, link, bond
e	Bedingung	condition, requirement
s	Bedürfnis	need, want, requirement
e	Beeinträchtigung	impairment, interference, intrusion
e	Befähigung	qualification
e	Befriedigung	satisfaction, gratification
e	Begierde	desire, lust
e	Behandlung	treatment, therapy, cure
e	Behauptung	statement, declaration, assertion
	e Selbstbehauptung	self-assertion, self-assertiveness
e	Beherrschung	domination, control, mastery
e	Beobachtung	observation
e	Bereitschaft	readiness, preparedness, tendency
e	Beschränkung	restriction, limitation, constraint
e	Besetzung	cathexis, cathection, charge
e	Bestimmung	determination, decision, destination
e	Bewältigung	coping, mastery
e	Bewegung	movement, agitation, emotion
e	Bewußtheit	attribute of being conscious, awareness
e	Bewußtmachung	process of making sth conscious
s	Bewußtsein	consciousness, awareness
s	Bewußtwerden	awareness
e	Bewußtwerdung	dawning of consciousness
e	Bindung	tie, binding, attachment
e	Deutung	interpretation
r	Drang (drängen)	urge, drive, desire (to push, press, urge)
e	Durchsetzung (sich durchsetzen)	carrying through, accomplishment, assertion (to assert oneself)

58

e	Eigenschaft	quality, attribute, property, trait
e	Einheit	unity, unit, entity
e	Einsicht	insight, understanding, discernment, perceptiveness
e	Einstellung	attitude, opinion, mental set
e	Empfindung	sensation, perception
e	Entfaltung	explication, growth, development
e	Entstehung	emergence, origination, genesis, formation
e	Entstellung	distortion, displacement
e	Entwicklung	development, evolution, developmental growth
e	Entziehung	detoxication, withdrawal, privation
s	Erbe (ererbt past part.)	heritage (inherited)
e	Erfahrung	experience
e	Erinnerung	memory
e	Erkrankung	disease, affection, illness, sickness
e	Erregung	excitement, agitation, excitation
r	Ersatz	substitute, replacement, surrogate
e	Erscheinung	phenomenon, apparition, manifestation, symptom
e	Erwerbung	acquisition
e	Erziehung	education, upbringing, rearing, training
	(anerzogen past part.)	(instilled)
e	Erzeugung	generation, reproduction, creation
s	Es	the Id, id
e	Fehlhandlung	parapraxis, abnormal action, faulty act
e	Fehlleistung	failure of action, faulty act, parapraxia
e	Flucht	escape, flight
e	Geburt (angeboren past part.)	birth, childbirth, delivery (innate, inborn, natural, inherited)
s	Gedächtnis	memory, mneme, recollection, remembrance
s	Gefühl	feeling, sentiment, emotion
	e Gefühlsregung	emotional impulse
	(cf. Regung)	
e	Gegenbesetzung	external counter cathexis
r	Geist	mind, spirit, wit, ghost
s	Geschlecht	sex, gender
e	Gestalt	gestalt, configuration, form, pattern
e	Gewalt	violence
s	Gewissen	conscience
r	Grenzfall	borderline case
e	Handlung	action, act, operation, performance
e	Hemmung	inhibition, suppression, inhibitedness
e	Herabsetzung	depreciation, detraction
s	Ich	ego
	e Ichspaltung	dissociation or splitting or division of the ego
	e Ichveränderung	alteration of the ego
s	Innere	interior

e	Kraft	strength, power, force vigour
e	Krankheit	illness, sickness, disease
s	Kranksein	state of being ill
s	Krankwerden	state of falling ill
s	Leiden	suffering, affliction, disease, disorder
e	Leistung	performance, accomplishment attainment, achievement
s	Leitbild	ideal, model, inner image
e	Lust ≠ Unlust	desire, pleasure, lust ≠ displeasure, unpleasure
r	Mangel	lack, deficiency, shortage
s	Merkmal	mark, feature, trait, characteristic
r	Minderwertigkeitskomplex	inferiority feeling or complex
e	Mischung (Entmischung) der Triebe	fusion (defusion) of instincts
e	Neigung	inclination, tendency, disposition
e	Phantasie	imagination, fantasy
e	Prägung	imprinting, imprint
e	Psyche	mind, psyche
e	Regung	emotion, impulse
r	Reiz	stimulus
r	Reizschutz	protection against external stimuli
e	Richtung	direction, trend
e	Schädigung	damage, impairment, injury
s	Schicksal	fate, fortune, destiny
r	Schlaf	sleep
r	Schlaftrieb	instinct to sleep
e	Schuld	guilt, fault
s	Schuldbewußtsein	consciousness, feeling or sense of guilt
s	Schuldgefühl	feeling or sense of guilt
e	Schwelle	limen, threshold
e	Seele (seelisch adj.)	soul, psyche, mind (mental, psychic, psychical)
s	Seelenleben	mental life, inner life
r	Selbsterhaltungstrieb	instinct of self-preservation
s	Sinnesorgan	sense organ
e	Spaltung	split, splitting, dissociation, division
e	Spannung	tension, stress, strain, tenseness
r	Stamm	tribe, race
e	Stauung	stasis
e	Stimmung	mood, humour, state of mind
e	Störung	disorder, disturbance, trouble, derangement
e	Strafe	punishment, penalty, withdrawal of reward

e	Strebung (streben nach)	striving, trend, aspiration (to strive, aspire, aim)
e	Stufe	step, stage, level, grade
e	Sucht	mania, addiction
r	Tagesrest	day residue, dream instigator
e	Tiefenpsychologie	depth psychology
e	Trauer	mourning
	e Trauerarbeit	working through bereavement
r	Traum	dream
	e Traumarbeit	dream work
	e Traumentstellung	dream distortion
	r Traumhintergrund	dream screen
	r Tagtraum	daydream
r	Trieb	instinct, drive, motive, urge
r	Triebanspruch	instinctual demand
s	Triebgeschehen	instinctual processes
e	Triebkraft	driving force, motive, impulse
e	Triebregung	instinctual impulse
e	Triebentmischung	defusion of instincts
e	Übereinstimmung	agreement, concordance, correspondence
s	Über-Ich	superego
e	Überlieferung	tradition, social transmission
e	Übertragung	transference, transfer transmission
e	Überwindung	overcoming, surmounting
e	Umgebung	environment, surroundings, milieu
s	Unbewußte	unconscious, unconscious mind, unconsciousness
s	Unterbewußte	subconscious
s	Unterbewußtsein	subconscious mind, subconsciousness
e	Unterdrückung	suppression
e	Untersuchung	investigation, examination, analysis
s	Urbild	archetype, prototype, imago
e	Ursache	cause
e	Urtümlichkeit	originality, naturalness
e	Veränderung	change, alteration, modification, transformation
e	Veranlagung	predisposition, disposition, constitutional tendency
e	Verdrängung	repression, suppression
e	Vererbung	inheritance, heredity
s	Verfahren	method, procedure, process
e	Verfolgung	persecution
	r Verfolgungswahn	delusion of persecution, persecution mania, complex
e	Vergangenheit	past
s	Verhalten	behaviour, conduct
s	Verhältnis	relationship, relation, proportion
e	Verinnerlichung	interiorization, internalization
e	Verkehrung	reversal
e	Verkörperung	personification, impersonation

r	Verlauf	course
s	Vermögen	faculty, power
e	Verschiebung	shift, move displacement (in particular by a dream)
e	Verstärkung	reinforcement, intensification
e	Verwerfung	rejection, dismissal
e	Verwirklichung	realization, materialization
s	Verzeihen	forgiveness, pardon
r	Verzicht	renunciation, resignation
s	Vorbewußte	preconscious, foreconscious
s	Vorbild	model, prototype, ideal
r	Vorgang	proceedings, event, process
s	Vorgehen	procedure, proceeding
e	Vorstellung	idea, notion, imagination, representation
r	Wahn	delusion, madness, mania
r	Wahnsinn	lunacy, insanity, madness, frenzy, mania
e	Wahnvorstellung	delusional idea, delusion
e	Wahrnehmung	perception
r	Widerstand	resistance, opposition, antagonism, blockage
s	Wirken (wirken)	work (to work, have an effect (on), be effective, act)
e	Wirkung	effect, impact
r	Wunsch	wish
e	Wunscherfüllung	wish fulfilment
e	Wunschvorstellung	wishful thinking
e	Zerstörung	destruction, ruin, ruination
e	Zielvorstellung	goal image, anticipatory imagination, purposive idea
r	Zug	trait
r	Zwang	compulsion, coercion, constraint, obsessive state
e	Zwangshandlung	obsessional or compulsive act
e	Zwangsneurose	compulsion neurosis, compulsive-obsessive neurosis, obsessional neurosis
e	Zwangsvorstellung	obsession, compulsive idea

10.3.   Words occurring frequently in sociology texts

s	Abendland	West, Occident
e	Abhängigkeit	dependency
e	Ableitung (ableiten)	derivation, deduction (to infer, derive, deduce)
e	Abnahme	decrease, reduction, decline, fall
s	Abreagieren (sich abreagieren)	abreaction, acting out
e	Allgemeinheit	(general) public, nation, community
e	Aneignung	appropriation
s	Angeborene (angeboren past part.)	that which is innate, inborn, natural

62

r	Angriff (angreifen)	attack, assault, aggression (to attack, assault)
e	Anpassung (sich anpassen)	assimilation (to assimilate)
r	Anspruch	claim, right, demand, pretension
r	Anstieg	rise, increase
e	Art	species, kind, sort, type
	e Arterhaltung	survival of the species
	e Artgenosse	person of the same type
e	Ausbeutung	exploitation
r	Ausgleich	compensation, balance
e	Auslese	selection
	auslösen	trigger, unleash, cause
r	Bedarf	need, want, requirements
e	Bedingung	condition, stipulation, requirement
s	Bedürfnis	need, want, requirement
e	Befähigung	qualifications, ability
e	Behauptung (sich behaupten)	assertion (to assert oneself)
	e Selbstbehauptung	self-assertion, self-assertiveness
e	Beherrschung	domination, mastery
e	Belastung	loading, burdening, strain
e	Bereitschaft	readiness, willingness, disposition
e	Beschränkung	restriction, limitation, constraint
r	Besitz (besitzen)	property, possession (to possess, own)
e	Bestimmung	determination, destination
	e Selbstbestimmung	self-determination
e	Bevölkerung	population
e	Bewegung	movement
e	Beziehung (sich beziehen auf)	relation (to refer to)
r	Bezug	relation, reference
	e Bezugsgruppe	reference group
	s Bezugsnetz	reference network
	e Bezugsperson	person to whom someone relates most closely
	r Bezugsrahmen	frame of reference
e	Bildung	education, formation
s	Böse	evil, harm
r	Drang	urge, drive
r	Druck	pressure
e	Duldsamkeit	tolerance
e	Duldung	toleration, allowance
e	Durchsetzung (sich durchsetzen)	carrying through, accomplishment, assertion (to assert oneself)
	eigen	own
	s Eigentum	property, ownership
e	Einrichtung	institution
e	Einschränkung	limitation, restriction, reduction
r	Einzelne	individual
s	Einzelwesen	individual
e	Entfremdung	alienation

e	Entstehung	emergence, origination, genesis, formation
e	Entwicklung	development, evolution, developmental growth
s	Erbe (ererbt past part.)	heritage (inherited)
e	Erduldung	endurance, sufferance
e	Erfahrung	experience
	erhalten	preserve, maintain
e	Erregung (erregen)	excitement, agitation, excitation (to excite, agitate)
r	Ersatz (ersetzen)	substitute, replacement (to replace, substitute)
e	Erwartung	expectation
r	Erwerb	acquisition, living, earnings
s	Erzeugnis	product
e	Erziehung (anerzogen past part.)	education, up-bringing (instilled)
s	Exemplar	specimen
e	Fähigkeit	ability, capability
e	Förderung (fördern)	encouragement, promotion, support (to promote, support)
e	Fortpflanzung	reproduction, spread
r	Fortschritt	progress
e	Gattung	type, kind, sort
r	Gebrauch	use, custom
	r Gebrauchswert	use-value
s	Gefüge	structure, framework, system
	gelten	to be valid, count, be worth
e	Gemeinschaft	community, society
e	Gesamtheit	whole, totality, entirety
s	Geschehen	happening, event
s	Geschlecht	sex, house, race, lineage
e	Gesellschaft	society
	e Vergesellschaftung	socialization, nationalization
e	Gestaltung	structuring
	e Umgestaltung	restructuring
e	Gleichheit	equality, likeness, identity
s	Gleichgewicht	equilibrium, balance
e	Gültigkeit	validity
e	Haltung	attitude
r	Handel	trade
e	Handlung	action, act, operation, performance
e	Herkunft	origin, birth, provenance
e	Herrschaft	rule, dominion, control
e	Lage	situation, position
s	Lebewesen	living thing
e	Leistung	performance, accomplishment, attainment, achievement
	r Leistungsdruck	pressure (to do well)
	e Leistungsgesellschaft	achievement-oriented society, meritocracy

64

s	Leitbild	ideal, model
s	Lernen (erlernt past part.)	learning (learned, learnt)
e	Lust ≠ Unlust	desire, pleasure ≠ displeasure, unpleasure
r	Mangel	lack, deficiency, shortage
r	Markt	market
e	Masse	the masses, crowd
	e Vermassung	loss of identity or individuality, massification
	r Massenmensch	mass man
e	Mehrheit	majority
s	Merkmal	mark, feature, trait, characteristic
e	Minderheit	minority
s	Mitglied	member
r	Mitmensch	fellow-man or creature
s	Mittel	means
	e Vermittlung (vermitteln)	mediation (to mediate)
e	Mündigkeit	majority, maturity, responsibility
s	Muster	model, pattern
e	Ordnung	order, system
r	Plan	plan, project
	e Planung	planning
e	Prägung	imprint, imprinting
e	Rangstellung	position in a hierarchy
e	Regung	emotion, impulse
r	Reiz	stimulus
s	Rollenverständnis	understanding / acceptance of a role one is playing
r	Rückgang	regression
e	Schädigung	harm, damage
e	Schicht	stratum, layer
e	Schwelle	limen, threshold
	r Schwellenwert	threshold or liminal value
e	Selbständigkeit (selbständig adj.)	independence, autonomy (independent, autonomous)
e	Spannung	tension, stress, strain
r	Stamm	tribe, race
	e Stammesgeschichte	phylogeny
r	Stand	station, status, rank position, class
r	Status	status, rank, position
e	Stauung	stasis
e	Stellung	position
e	Stimmung	mood, sentiment
e	Stufe	level, rank, grade
r	Tausch	exchange
	r Tauschwert	exchange-value

e	Trägheit	sluggishness, slowness
r	Trieb	instinct, drive, motive, urge
r	Überbau	superstructure
e	Überlieferung	tradition, social transmission
e	Umgebung	surroundings, background
r	Umschwung	reversal, drastic change
e	Umwelt	environment
r	Umstand	circumstance
r	Urteil	judgement, opinion
s	Vorurteil	prejudice
e	Veränderung	transformation, change, alteration, modification
e	Verbreitung (sich verbreiten)	spreading, dissemination, propagation (to spread, propagate (itself))
e	Vererbung (vererbt past part.)	inheritance, heredity (inherited)
s	Verhalten (sich verhalten)	behaviour, conduct (to behave)
r	Verhaltensforscher	behaviourist
e	Verhaltensforschung	behaviourism
e	Verhaltensweise	behaviour pattern, mode of behaviour
s	Verhältnis	relationship, relation, proportion
	die Verhältnisse (pl.)	conditions, circumstances
r	Verlauf	course
e	Vermehrung	increase, augmentation, growth, multiplication
e	Verständigung	communication
s	Verständnis	understanding
e	Verteilung	distribution
e	Voraussetzung	prerequisite, requirement
s	Vorbild	model, prototype, ideal
r	Vorgang	proceedings, event, process
s	Vorgehen	procedure, proceeding
e	Wahl	choice, election
e	Auswahl	selection
e	Weise	way, manner, fashion
r	Wert	value
e	Werthaftigkeit	validity, quality of value
e	Verwertung	utilization, exploitation
e	Wirkung (wirken)	effect, impact (to work, have an effect on, act)
e	Einwirkung	influence, impact
e	Auswirkung	consequence, effects result, repercussion
	bewirken	to cause, bring about, produce
s	Ziel	goal, aim, objective
r	Zug	trait, tendency
e	Zunahme	increase, augmentation
r	Zustand	state, condition
r	Zweck	purpose, aim

Index

Bibliography

Wolfgang Fleischer: Wortbildung der deutschen Gegenwartssprache, Niemeyer 1975 (VEB Leipzig)
Francine Saucier: Grammaire Allemande, Paris: Bordas 1985
François Schanen, Jean Paul Confais: Grammaire de l'allemand, formes et fonctions, Paris: Fernand Nathan 1986
Dora Schulz, Heinz Griesbach: Grammatik der deutschen Sprache, München: Hueber 1982
Jacqueline Trometer, Henri Courtade, André Kleefeld: Nouvelle grammaire allemande, Paris: Fernand Nathan 1984
Hubert Eichheim, Barbara Momenteau, Ulrich Olschewsky, Dietrich Sturm: L'allemand clés en main, München: Langenscheidt 1986
Jean Laplanche et Jean Baptiste Pontalis: Vocabulaire de la Psychanalyse, Paris: Presses Universitaires de France 1981

For further reference

Herbert Lederer: Reference Grammar of the German Language, New York: Charles Scribner's Sons 1990 (1969)
A. E. Hammer: German Grammar Usage, London: Edward Arnold (Hodder & Stoughton) 1989 (1971)